MW00902273

I AM WORTHY OF LUXURY LOVE, LUXURY LIFESTYLE AND LUXURY MINDSET!

MY BLACK IS LUXURY.

I AM BEAUTIFUL AND BREATHTAKING.

I EMBRACE THE GREATNESS WITHIN ME.

I AM FILLED WITH JOY, HAPPINESS, AND LOVE.

I AM ATTRACTING WEALTH AND ABUNDANCE IN MY LIFE.

I AM SO MUCH MORE THAN I THOUGHT I COULD BE.

I HAVE EVERYTHING I NEED TO BE HAPPY RIGHT NOW.

I AM NOW A REFLECTION OF MY HIGHEST SELF.

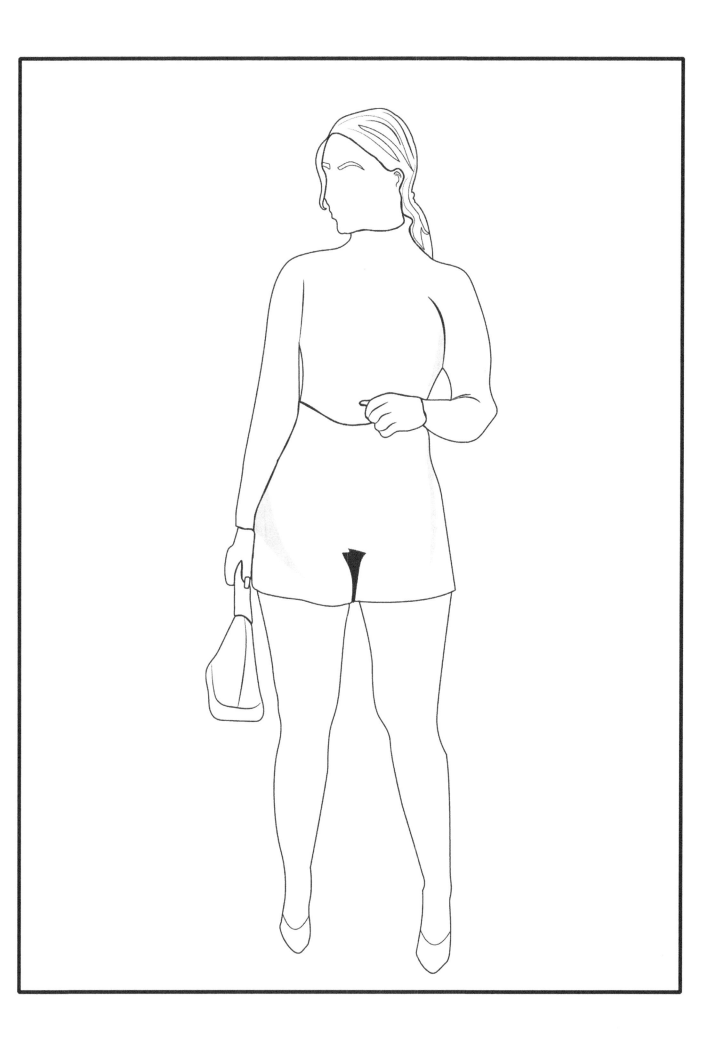

I TREAT MY SELF-LOVE AS THE VIP SECTION.

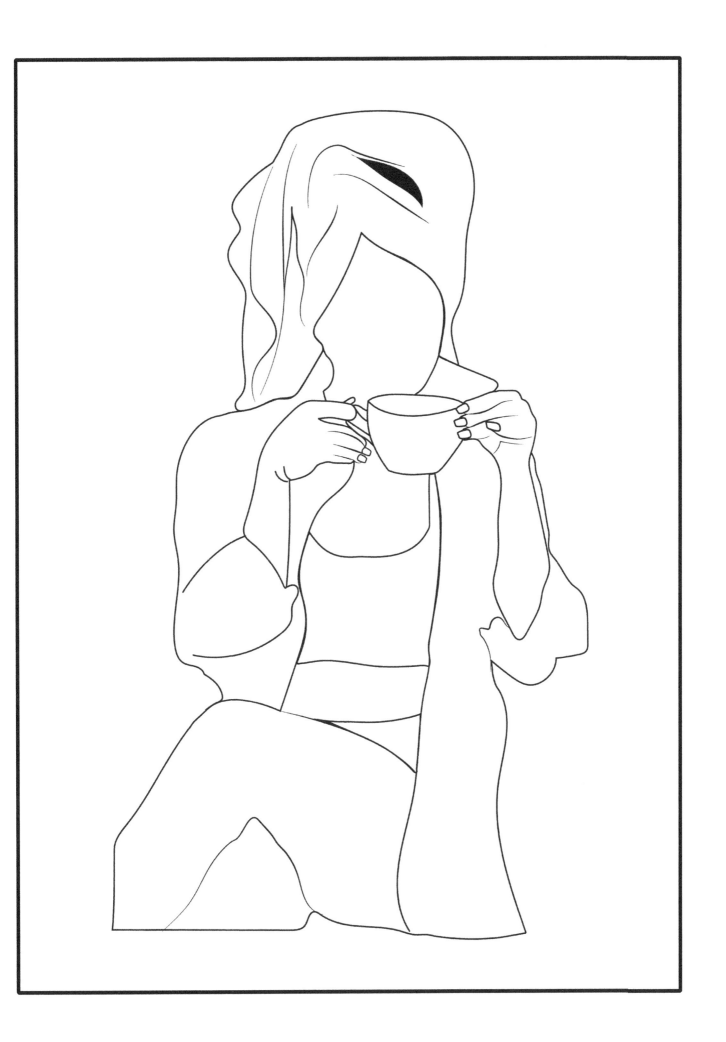

I AM LOVED BY GOD AND HE CALLS ME BEAUTIFUL.

BLACK GIRL - PERIOD.

I AM
STYLE & GRACE.

I AM BLOSSOMING INTO THE BEST VERSION OF MYSELF.

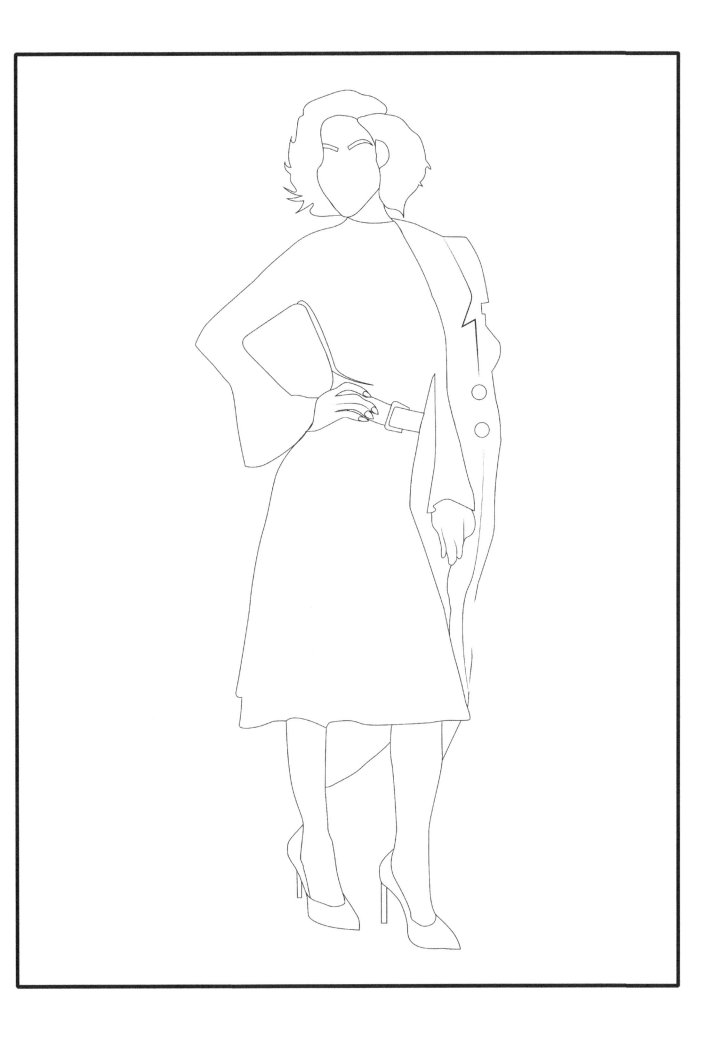

I AM WORTHY OF LOVE & HAPPINESS.

I AM SUCCESSFUL AT EVERYTHING I DO.

I ACCEPT AND LOVE MYSELF, JUST THE WAY I AM.

I AM BECOMING THE CHANGE I WANT TO SEE.

I AM BECOMING THE CHANGE I WANT TO SEE.

I AM WORTHY OF LUXURY LOVE, LUXURY LIFESTYLE AND LUXURY MINDSET!

MY BLACK IS LUXURY.

I AM BEAUTIFUL AND BREATHTAKING.

I EMBRACE THE GREATNESS WITHIN ME.

I AM FILLED WITH JOY, HAPPINESS, AND LOVE.

I AM ATTRACTING WEALTH AND ABUNDANCE IN MY LIFE.

I AM SO MUCH MORE THAN I THOUGHT I COULD BE.

I HAVE EVERYTHING I NEED TO BE HAPPY RIGHT NOW.

I AM NOW A REFLECTION OF MY HIGHEST SELF.

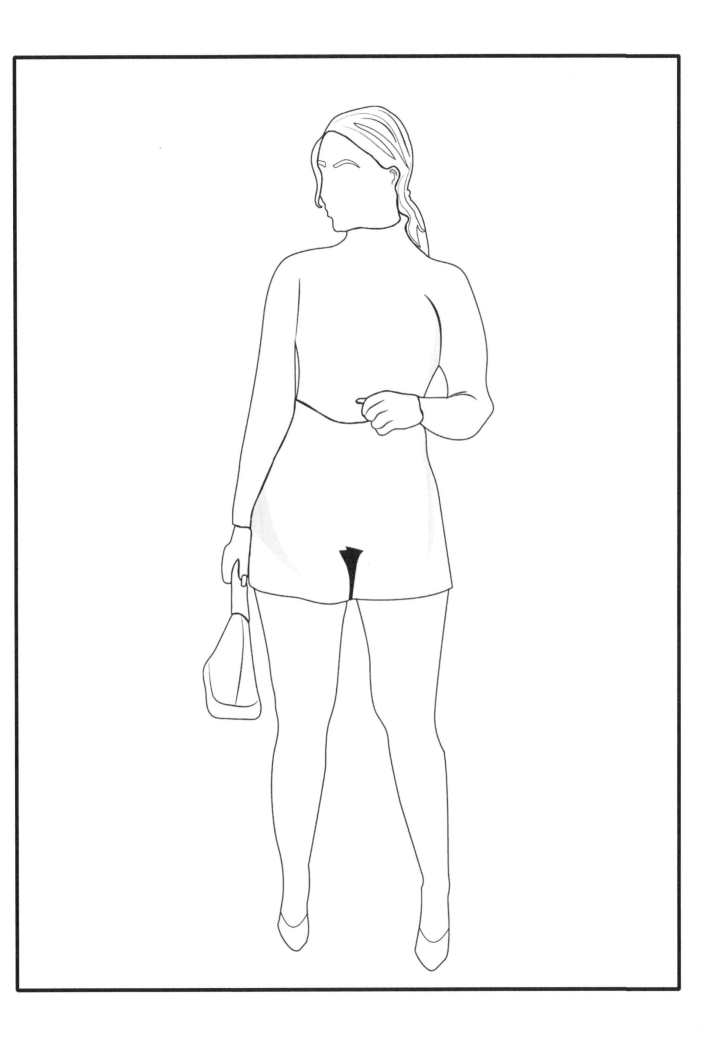

I TREAT MY SELF-LOVE AS THE VIP SECTION.

I AM LOVED BY GOD AND HE CALLS ME BEAUTIFUL.

BLACK GIRL - PERIOD.

I AM
STYLE & GRACE.

I AM BLOSSOMING INTO THE BEST VERSION OF MYSELF.

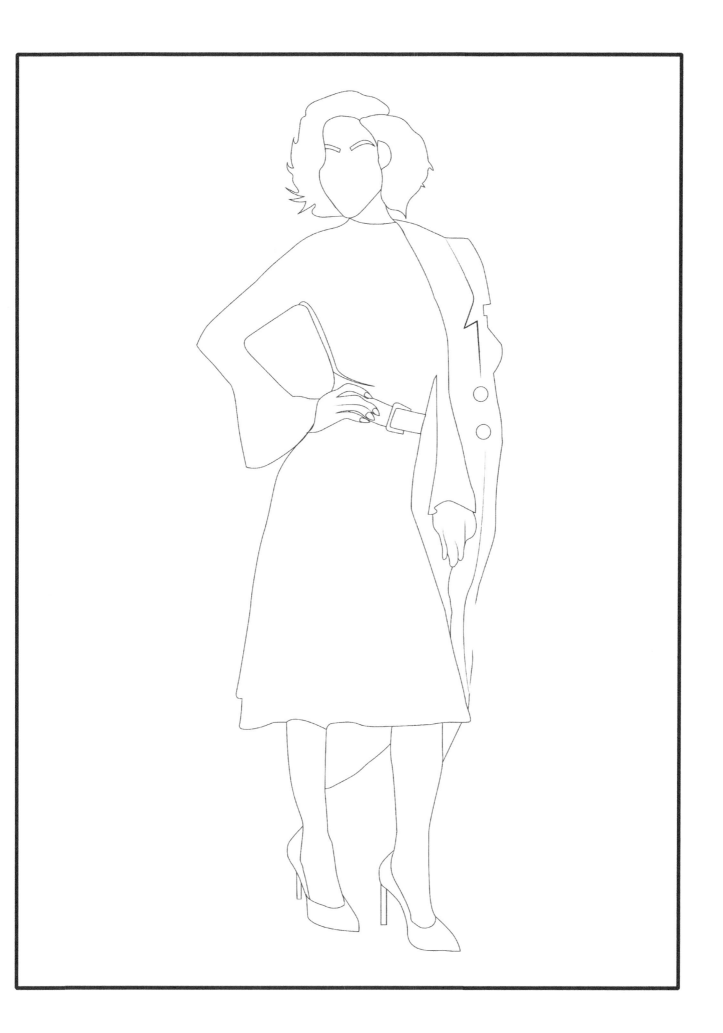

I AM WORTHY OF LOVE & HAPPINESS.

I AM SUCCESSFUL AT EVERYTHING I DO.

I ACCEPT AND LOVE MYSELF, JUST THE WAY I AM.

I AM BECOMING THE CHANGE I WANT TO SEE.

I AM BECOMING THE CHANGE I WANT TO SEE.

I AM WORTHY OF LUXURY LOVE, LUXURY LIFESTYLE AND LUXURY MINDSET!

MY
BLACK IS
LUXURY.

I AM BEAUTIFUL AND BREATHTAKING.

I EMBRACE THE GREATNESS WITHIN ME.

I AM FILLED WITH JOY, HAPPINESS, AND LOVE.

I AM ATTRACTING WEALTH AND ABUNDANCE IN MY LIFE.

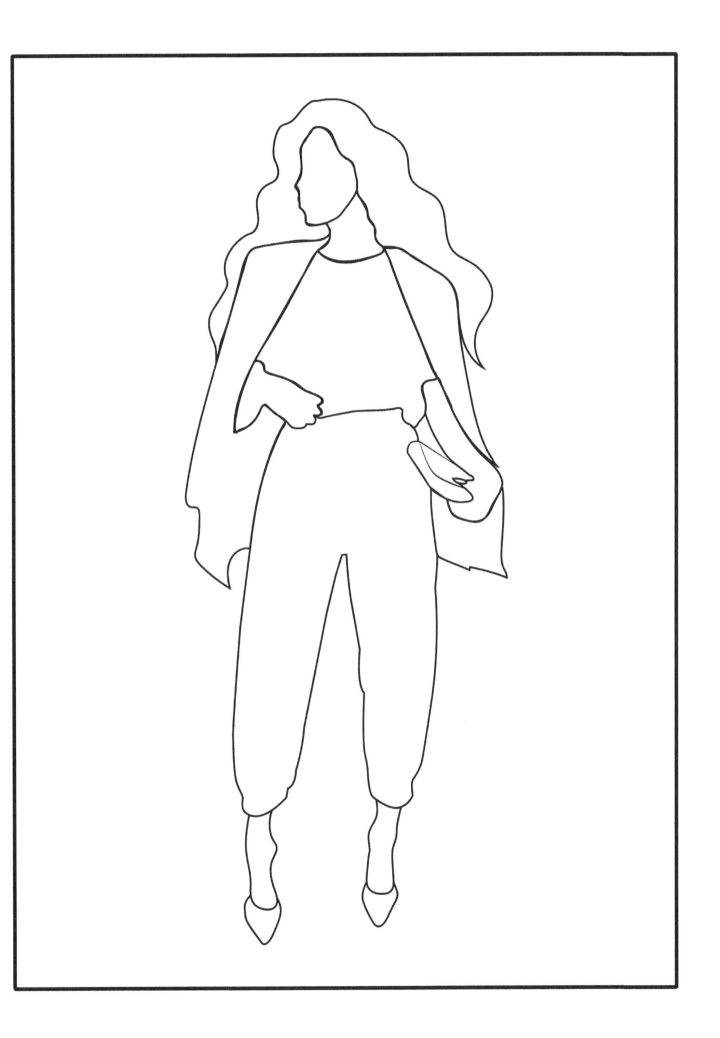

I AM SO MUCH MORE THAN I THOUGHT I COULD BE.

I HAVE EVERYTHING I NEED TO BE HAPPY RIGHT NOW.

I AM NOW A REFLECTION OF MY HIGHEST SELF.

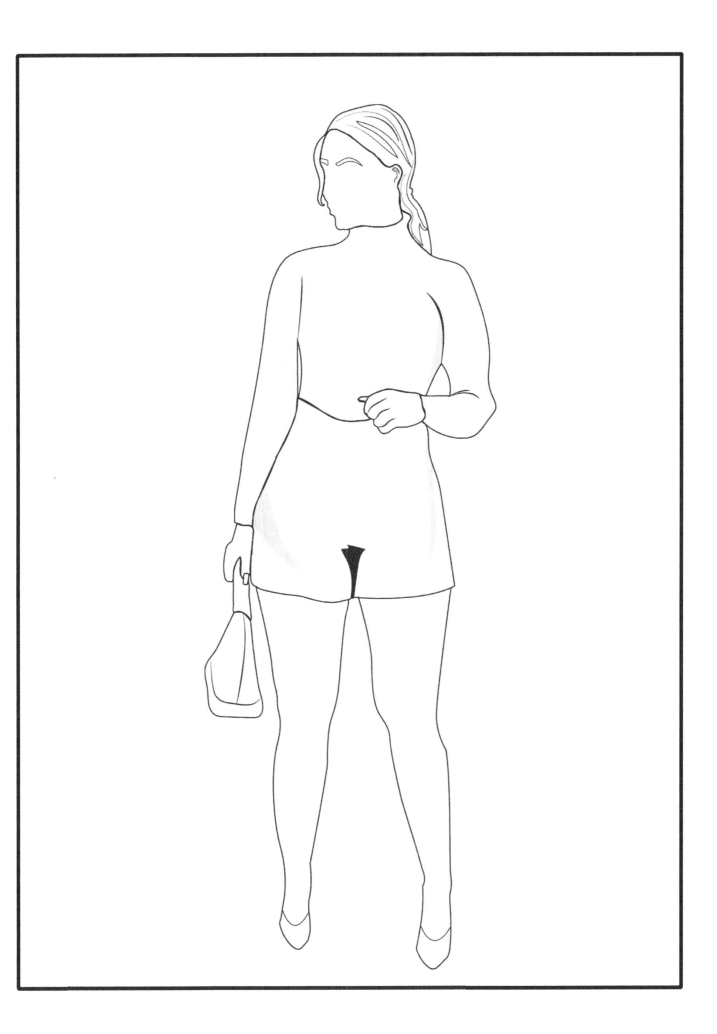

I TREAT MY SELF-LOVE AS THE VIP SECTION.

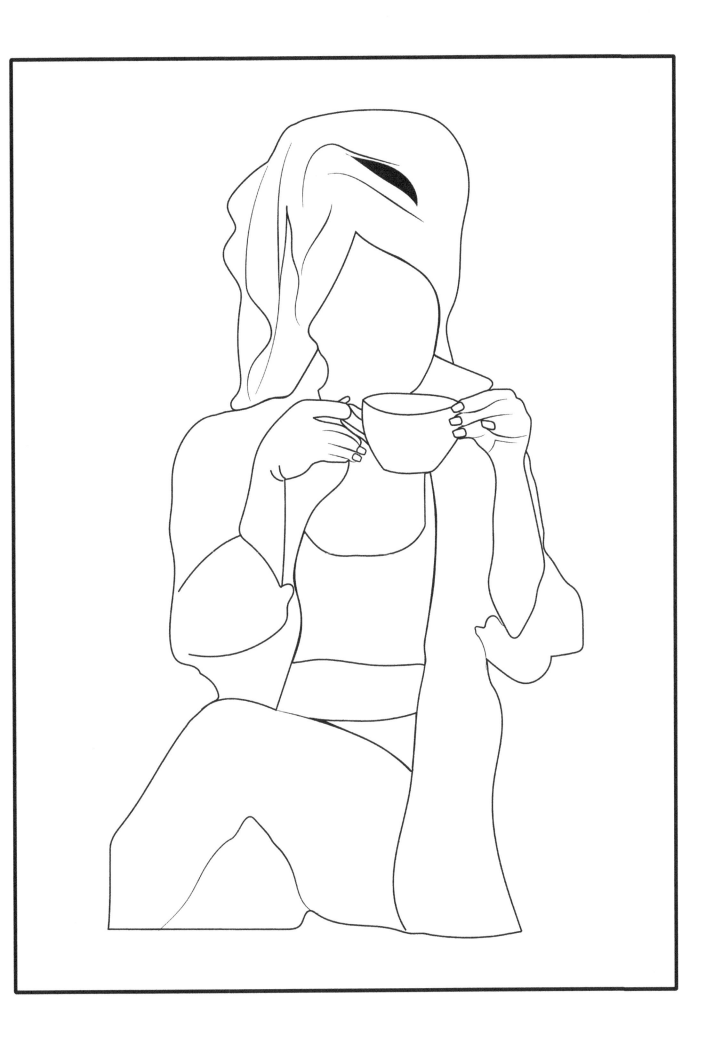

I AM LOVED BY GOD AND HE CALLS ME BEAUTIFUL.

BLACK GIRL - PERIOD.

I AM
STYLE & GRACE.

I AM BLOSSOMING INTO THE BEST VERSION OF MYSELF.

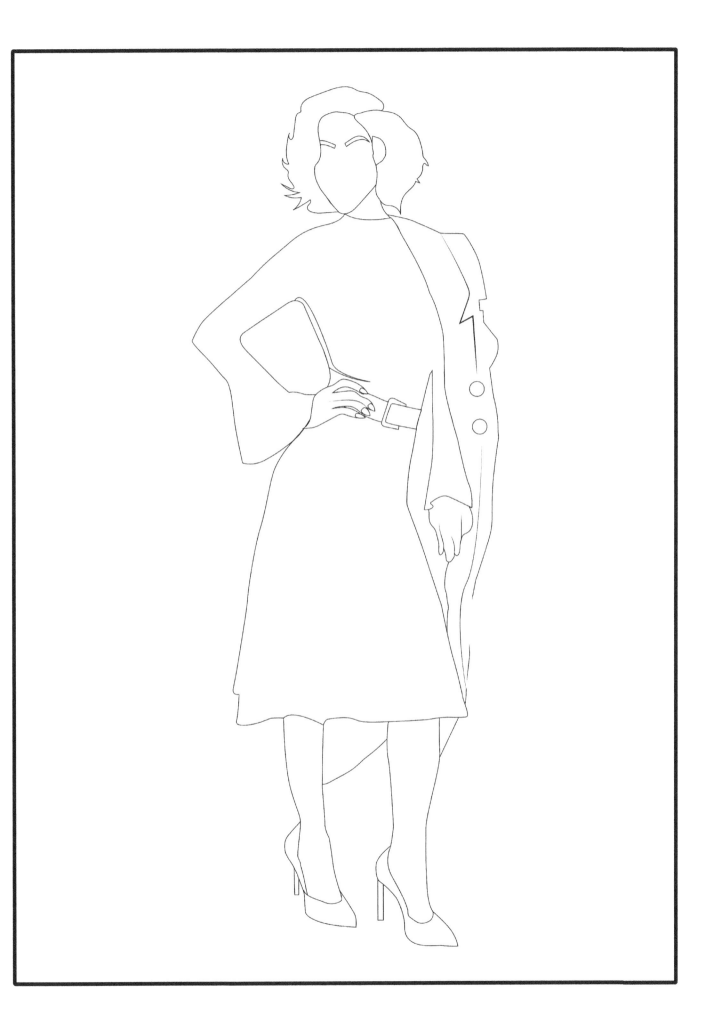

I AM WORTHY OF LOVE & HAPPINESS.

I AM SUCCESSFUL AT EVERYTHING I DO.

I ACCEPT AND LOVE MYSELF, JUST THE WAY I AM.

I AM BECOMING THE CHANGE I WANT TO SEE.

I AM BECOMING THE CHANGE I WANT TO SEE.

Made in the USA
Las Vegas, NV
08 November 2023